MW00884755

It Only Hurts
When I Rhyme

It Only Hurts When I Rhyme

Tarzana Joe

To order additional copies of this book, contact:
Xlibris LLC
1-888-795-4274
www.Xlibris.com
Orders@Xlibris.com
142668

CONTENTS

Poet's Notes 11
Editorial Reply 13
To Those Who Compare Human Tragedy
    To Invertebrate Extinctions 16
Chapel 17
Cuidado! 18
Hockey Heaven 20
Autism Speaks 22
Dedication Of The City Of Rosemead 9/11 Memorial 24
4 Questions On 9/11 25
Some Consequences Of The Affordable Care Act 26
Embarrassment Of Riches 28
New Media 29
Bucket List 30
Tides 32
A Poet In Hollywood 33
Best TV Ever? 35
Fun With Phonics 36
Animals And Politics 37
Congress Reconvenes 38
A Song For Tough Times 39
Everything You Know Is Wrong 41
Labor Day 42
Memorial Day On Wilshire Blvd 43
Reason For The Season 44
Branches 46
A Holiday Epiphany 48
Happy New Year 49
Election Day 1 50
Election Day 2 51
Seal Team Six 53

A Moment Of Silence, Please..54
You Don't Say..55
Gentle On My Mind 57
A Refusal To Answer..59
A Pile Of Promises 60
Does Genius Get A Pass?..61
Fight On!..62
Loose Change..63
No Strings..64
Away With Words..65
Howz That Again?...67
The President's Report Card 68
A Ban On Banning..70
And Regulations 72
Stimulus 2 Or "This Time, Fer Sure" 74
Blame Me 76
Oops...77
Thoughts At 28 79
In The Aftermath Of The Boston Marathon Bombing.......................80
Thoughts At 37 82
In The Aftermath Of The Navy Shooting 83
Thoughts At 49 84

DEDICATION

I had a calling, always knew it
But never had the will to do it
The years raced past, I almost blew it
Then came the fetching Mrs. Hewitt

While many met my words with curses
Declared my poems should ride in hearses
Or have their chests be thumped by nurses
Alone, she praised my humble verses

She said, "Don't read the poems of others...
I'll take your words, had I my druthers...
Ascend the heights where genius wuthers...
Join Blake and Keats and all them brothers."

So every week, I seek the muses
And write a poem from where the news is
(The last five minutes after "who-ziz")
And then I'll get to go on cruises

And in this pseudonymic guise
Should my poetic fortunes rise.
It's Mrs. H. I'll recognize
When I accept the Nobel Prize

OH, yes... and for my wife and son, too!

Poetry is ordered thought. In a world made more random by search engines and falling stars, poetry is not a luxury; it is as important as a good multi-vitamin. As the pace of life quickens, many species have lost the ability to think before they speak. Among the pundits, it's survival of the glibbest. No wonder the level of discourse has dropped below the fifth parking sub-basement.

The poet, by definition, must think before he speaks. He usually takes additional time for some old scotch and a nice cigar before he speaks. During the lull, he is forced by his craft to find precisely the right words to make his point. It's not only the rhyming words that he must find ... but all the little words that go between them if he is to follow the structure he has set for himself. I could list the various metric forms and rhyme schemes here as examples, but the only one I know for certain without looking it up is the Limerick and you all know that one.

The goal of the poet is to connect with his reader over thousands of miles or hundreds of years. The poem is a transporter and a time machine. The power source for these amazing appliances is the common core of humanity. Like any writer, the poet must convince himself that what has just occurred to him has crossed the minds of a million people before without having been put down on paper. The poet then expresses that thought so his readers will recognize it as their own.

I rhyme because I have to. When the thought concludes with a good rhyme, it becomes more amusing, profound and memorable. And memory is the key. In order for civilization to grow, mankind had to pass down knowledge to the next generation. In the centuries before spoken language evolved into written language, essential information had to be committed to memory. It wasn't the wheel or agriculture that built civilizations; it was the invention of rhyme.

So I invite you to read the poems herein contained for enjoyment and inspiration. I would be delighted too, if you would commit one or more to memory.

Tarzana Joe

POET'S NOTES

Many of the poems that follow were inspired by the news of the week in which they were written. Where necessary, I will attempt to conjure up the context in an introductory paragraph. But what to start with? I'll start with a poem that is my personal favorite.

Soon after 9/11, when the world chorus of sympathy had subsided, intellects and editorial writers around the country concluded that the United States was again despised by the rest of the world. They reached this conclusion despite the clear evidence of the millions who seek to move here and live here. They listed as the valid reasons for this hatred our historic oppression of native peoples and participation in the slave trade. Clearly no other country on earth had such a history. But they went further. Our current consumerism and standard of living were equally valid reasons—not for emulation or even envy—but for justified hatred. One particularly fine editorial was published in the Minneapolis Star Tribune and inspired this poem.

EDITORIAL REPLY

Oh, say can you see, the American Dream
The world holds you in low esteem
Your image has gone down to ruin
According to the Star Tribune
(ditto in the Daily Bruin)

Just so you understand it fully
In plainest words, you are a bully
To those who loathe and say they hate you
And desperately imitate you.

In world affairs, you play too rough
Your taxes aren't high enough
Your preferences are so plebeian
Your tastes, not up to European

Your diplomats, those kooks and haters
Refuse to schmooze with mad dictators
Those diplomats, who, entre nous
Can barely say, merci beaucoup
Have made us look like so much vermin
Just like I heard in last week's sermon.

Why can't you be a better sport
And show the world some more support
With policies that aim to please
Just like the Communist Chinese?

Who sign whatever's put before 'em
Then promptly go on to ignore 'em
Accords that serve the commonweal
Outlawing fur coats and veal
Limiting lint and water vapor
Boy, those sure look good on paper.

Why don't we sign whatever's next
Regardless of what's in the text
And put our pens without delay
To the Protocol on Tooth Decay

For, to be sure, the thing we lack
Is a worldwide policy on plaque
Oh, don't you see, what should unite us
Is the common threat of gingivitis?
And everything would sure be dandy
If America stopped making candy.

The nose of the world is out of joint
So let's assume they have a point
I've given serious consideration
To the current allied situation.

If we do these things that I outline
Our public image should be fine.

We should—America take note—
Give everyone the right to vote
We should let every preacher preach
And allow all men their own free speech

We should protect—now can't you guess
A good, non-partisan, free press
And welcome famished lads and lasses
Or send our troops to save their masses

And be, for the world, if you will
A shining city on a hill.

If we do these things then we'll have won 'em.
Goodness! We've already done them.

When I was a lad, I cried. You see,
A little boy wouldn't play with me.

My father, who was very clever.
Said these words I'll note forever.

"My son, I swear by God above you.
You can not make another love you.
I'll be the best that I can be
And trust good hearts will come to me."

Some day I'll write on his memorial
My dad's words crushed that editorial

If you purchased this book because you heard me on the radio, I would like to begin this collection with some poems you wouldn't have heard on the radio. They are a part of "a little private poetry" as Mel Brooks calls it.

TO THOSE WHO COMPARE HUMAN TRAGEDY TO INVERTEBRATE EXTINCTIONS

I am bigger than the earth
I can reach the farthest, faintest star in just a moment with my mind
I can reach the closeness of compassion with my heart
And that doesn't even account for where I'm going with my soul.

I am not ashamed of my dominion
And I will name names

I have sympathy for the ant on which I tread
And the elephant lost to ivory lust
Though they have none for me
They can have none for me
Because they lack the spark
The dinosaurs are gone and even though I had no hand in that
I gave them their names and I miss them

I study
I work
I father
I mother
I love

A thousand suns have shrunk and crashed since I've been born
And one is dying now
But still I live

So when I die
Mourn for me
For I am bigger than the earth

CHAPEL

Their sister died and they know what's next.
Their eyes are wet and soft with tears and age
And they know what's next

Another gathering of flowers
Another gathering of friends
Advent ends. Lent ends.

The room is empty now
But it will fill again
With younger men
And younger men will lose their lovely sisters

CUIDADO!

I started the day with a dangerous thought
"What if I don't go to work today?"
I would be a day behind in my overwhelming job.
I would be thought poorly of by my employer
I would have less money. (I get paid by the hour.)

I did not think for a moment that a little innocent hooky
During which I hoped to play some marital nookie
Would see my car rear-ended at the stop sign on the end of my street
Would see me strapped to a body board
Would see me looking at the ceiling of an ambulance for the first time in my life

In the ambulance, the paramedic asked what medications I was on.

Diovan HCL and Norvasc for blood pressure
Colchicine for the gout—a side effect of the blood pressure pills
Nexium for the chronic heartburn—a side effect of the Colchicine
Oh, and Zetia for high cholesterol
He suggested that I buy juice pills from his wife.

I started the day with a dangerous hope
I wanted the day to be different from the last 365
On the way home from family movie night
I saw a young driver making a left-hand turn
Clip a slight Asian girl who spun through the air
Like an extra in a Hong Kong movie
Perhaps she had been an extra in a Hong Kong movie
Because when I went to see if she was all right, she was.

I had a dangerous thought
Instead of juice pills, I wanted Jack in the Box
Who would have thought, while munching on my Chicken Ciabatta
That I would see a sign
That the sign would answer my questions
That the sign would inspire a poem, this poem
Cuidado! Piso Mojado!

Danger. The floor is dangerous.
The FLOOR is dangerous.
It's slippery when wet
Just like the street where I live
The job that I have
The earth under my feet

Cuidado! Piso mojado, people.

HOCKEY HEAVEN

I remember it so clearly
As if it were tomorrow
On the best day of December
Seven from the end
(I was eleven)
And a soft snow began to fall as daylight disappeared
And we could see, my friends and I,
That this was no ordinary snow
No, this was perfect, packing snow
The kind that comes only once or twice in a childhood
The kind that made monstrous snowmen
(You know that snow)
The kind that didn't stick to gloves or melt through mittens
It made baseball-size snowballs with ease
Ones that could be tossed with pinpoint accuracy
At telephone poles or kids from the next street

And this same snow, when tromped down by bald, buckled galoshes
Made our dead end street into a hockey rink
No skates—just sliding boots and sneakers.
And we played that night
By streetlight
As the TV-special snow dusted down
Hockey between the curbstones
Hockey between the trashcan goalposts
And we never rested
And we never tired
Way past our bedtimes
And we're playing still
And our parents never called us in
As if they sensed the perfection of
That snow
That game
That night

And if you are eleven
(Or ever were eleven)
Then this, my friends, is heaven
This, my friends, is heaven.
And those of you who doubt
The things you knew at seven
Then this is proof of heaven
This is proof of heaven

And, oh, my friends back then
Bruce and Ray and Kevin
Remember this with me
When we all return to heaven.

AUTISM SPEAKS

I think of Will, singing.
A special boy I know
Who, when I met him first
Hid behind his father's leg
And wailed when cars went by
Afraid in ways we didn't understand
And there he is today
Singing for his class
Filling the schoolyard and his
Father's heart with music.

And Adam
I think about the time
I stood beside him in the dim-lit room
Looking at the Star-Spangled Banner
He told me things the docent didn't know
Amazing tourists in the way
Another special boy
Confounded scholars in Jerusalem
Troubling His mother's heart

I think of Max
Who wouldn't speak
And always read the floor
And wondered when
I'd hear his voice
And there he is, sixteen
Walking, determined, to the bus stop.
I honk as I drive by and he waves

They seem so far away
The days when I first met them
And the journey has been hard
And the journey isn't over
And the journey doesn't end
As every parent knows

So, of course, I want to cry
But when I want to cry
I think of Will, singing

On the tenth anniversary of the most horrible day in the life of a country, the City of Rosemead dedicated a memorial to the fallen and to Rosemead firefighters who flew to New York to help in the rescue effort on 9/12. The sculpture depicts hands crafted from aluminum doves holding aloft an actual girder from the World Trade Center. I was honored to be a small part of the commemoration.

DEDICATION OF THE CITY OF ROSEMEAD 9/11 MEMORIAL

Not just the steel
That strength and courage built
and one man dared to cross
Astonishing the world
With beauty and bravado

Not just the steel
That stood for years
That stood for work and trade and peace
That greeted all
Who came to see the city and the Lady

The Lady stood with steel
And steel behind her stood
Shielding and upholding
Both liberty and freedom with her fire

Not just the steel
That fell that day
Twisted and confused by hate
A monument
To chaos and to evil
That frantic hands tore back
To find a breathing bit of life

Not just the steel
But every molecule of hope and soul and heart
Is resurrected and remade
Here
A continent away
A monument to life
Carried by bravery
To bring
Without fear or anger . . . Memory

4 QUESTIONS ON 9/11

Spring will never come again
No April without pain
Each April the Emancipator's
Slain

Mothers, will there ever
Be a Sunday in December
When we will not
Remember

November never passes
Until I shed a tear
Year after Year after Year

And never in September
Will I look into the sky
Without asking the question
Why Why Why Why

I think we need a break from serious poetry for a while. Let's get to
what I try to do every week at "five minutes to Friday night"

SOME CONSEQUENCES OF THE AFFORDABLE CARE ACT

We long have heard that poet's tale
A kingdom lost for want of nail
The lesson that should give us pause is
We can't foresee disasters' causes
An insect wing that stirs the breeze
Can bring a planet to its knees
Thus the threat of last week's vote is
Something we will hardly notice

A somewhat pale and sober man
Won't pay the tax. Won't get the tan
And feeling down and somewhat pallid
Won't think his hopes for love are valid
And never speak what's in his heart
And watch his dreamed-of wife depart
Because he skipped that tanning bed
His DNA and hers didn't wed
And on a dark and dreary morn
The second Einstein won't be born

What other cause for consternation
Is buried in this legislation?

The greatest of potential groaners
Is facing chefs and café owners
For every choice that's on their menu
In each and every eating venue
Yes, every dish, sautéed or roasted
Must have its health statistics posted
Exactly as the law advises
Precisely based on portion sizes
And if the law's enforced this way
It means the death of the buffet

Where government prescribes the meat
But surely not, "All you can eat"

Oppressive bill! And so rewardless
To make the future Smorgasbordless

It must be scrapped
It can't be mended
Or with a whimper
All is ended
From consequences, unintended.

EMBARRASSMENT OF RICHES

Each week I pen some verses
Evoking cheers or curses
About virtues or vices
Or some impending crisis
And I'd love to share my views
But there's nothing in the news

All politics is dandy
No governors are randy
The economy is jelling
And SUV's are selling
Sure, I'd love to sing my song
But not a thing is going wrong

No planets are aligning
Free agents aren't signing
No aliens are landing
Or Senators grandstanding
Something better happen soon
Because there's nothing to lampoon

Minnesotans aren't wrangling
Not a single chad is dangling
Anarchists aren't rioting
Oprah isn't dieting
The nightly news is such a bore
Nothing happens here no more

The market's doing peachy
The Pope is reading Nietzsche
Bless my soul and damn my eyes
There's not a thing to satirize

And yet each week I pen an ode
From my desk in my abode

This I've worried day and night about
There's not a single thing to write about

NEW MEDIA

(Apologies to Thomas Gray)
The sunset tolls the knell of mainstream news
The lowing herd once followed by the crowd
The editor who forced his leftist views
The analyst, once numbered with the proud

For them no more the blazing hearth of choice
Or busy housewife tunes to Channel 2
No children run to Uncle Walter's voice
No main stream maven tells them what to do

No more ye vain! Ye sycophants of power
No lion share of notice may you hog
Your day is in its final hour
The paths of glory lead but to the blog.

BUCKET LIST

There are life coaches who insist
That each of us should make a list
Of places fair and meals exquisite
That we intend to eat or visit
Of all the things we want to do
Before our days on earth are through

Perhaps this is some sound advice
Don't get me wrong—such lists are nice
But not as worthwhile undertaking
Or helpful as the list I'm making
I'm writing down; before I die
A list of things I'll never try

So heed my words, if you're disposed to
And hear the things I won't get close to

I won't attend an L.A. rave
Or spelunk in a bat-filled cave

I won't conspire with any crooks
Or tell my wife how THAT dress looks

I won't draw three cards to a flush
Or Facebook with a High School crush

Or turn away when someone needs me
Or ever bite the hand that feeds me

I won't decline a fine cigar
Or let Mel Gibson drive my car

Or try to burn a book that's holy
Or double-dip in guacamole

Or play a proper noun in Scrabble
Or ever miss a day of Drabble

Or ever cuss my dear old Granny
Or let Ms. Allred near my nanny

Or (this is how the poem ends)
Let Bob Woodward near my friends

Poems should call to mind the collective knowledge of a civilization. When Shakespeare wrote a play or a poem, he shoveled in as many references from his fine education that he could. And everybody in the audience knew what he meant (even the groundlings—who caught on after a few performances). They didn't have footnotes. Think of that, characters out of ancient epics! Moments in history that paralleled the crises in his characters' lives! Biblical quotations! And half of the great books weren't even written yet. Of course, the educational reforms of the 1970s replaced common knowledge with diversity. Why can't we have both?

TIDES

King Canute, man of war
Master of all he saw
Standing on the sandy shore
King Canute wanted more

Said Canute to the sea
Not another inch, said he
But despite his decree
Water up above his knee

King Canute, eye of dread
Didn't you hear a word I said?
Soon Canute turned and fled
Water up above his head

Take Canute as your guide
Though he ruled far and wide
Damply, he sat down and cried
Victim of the sin of pride
No man can command the tide

And Joshua, who stopped the sun
Who had all Canaan on the run
He had help from Number One
Does the global warming crew
Think that they can do it too?

Think again of that king
And this warning song I sing
All the congressmen you bring
Can't cool off that solar thing.

A POET IN HOLLYWOOD

Some nights after the meat loaf
Before the bill collector phones
I fancy that I live my life as
Tarzaniana Jones

I imagine midnight voyages
To drear and dark locales
Sharing "conversation" with
Exotic femme fatales
I'm toppling the tyrannies
Of potentate and Pasha
Gleefully outwitting every
Boris and Natasha
By day, I'm teaching coeds
Like any dashing poet
By night, instead, I'm saving
Civ'lization, as we know it.

But suddenly the fantasy
Unravels without warning
Instead of arks, I'm searching for
My glasses in the morning
Instead of excavating where
Those crystal skulls are lost
I'm digging in my savings for
What orthodontists cost.
Not brandishing a saber
Or administering the lash
I'm finishing the dishes
And I'm taking out the trash

Someday I may just race with
All those cattle in Pamplona
Till then for me, a special ops
Is treatment for glaucoma

I been around enough to know
Where fantasy begins
The villains are all bumblers
The hero always wins
I'll leave it up to Tinseltown
I've naught to be afraid of
My Hollywood Adventure
It's the stuff that dreams are made of

BEST TV EVER?

Ah, I see through the cathode, dully
Matlock, Rockford, Fox and Scully . . .

Every cop and every villain
Captain Kirk and Marshall Dillon
To each of you, of them I sing
Columbo, Jack McCoy, Sky King
The best show ever on TV?
Well, if the choice were up to me
I'd pick the show without a script
Not from the headlines, was this ripped
No writers or director paid
It was this show that headlines made
Acting class, they never took
Or studied Stanislavsky's book
The leading man? He did just fine
Although he flubbed his only line
My choice for greatest broadcast ever
You've guessed it—if you're really clever
The stars that have so much appeal
Their names, of course, are Buzz and Neil
For kindly, please, my logic follow.
Without TV, there's no Apollo
Without a place where we could tune
We'd never venture for the moon.
And though Von Braun conquered the air
Philo Farnsworth brought US there

Yes, we went through the cathode, brightly
To the wondrous orb, I gaze at, nightly.

FUN WITH PHONICS

Allow me to tell you a foly hable
The story of brothers, Ain and Cable
Now Cable lived life serene and mellow
But Ain was an angry and fealous jello

Ain wanted everything Even Steven
Just like their parents Ad and Even
But Cable had things a bittle letter
While Ain stitched up fig leaves, he swit a netter

Soon Cable's slood ran in the boil
Ain shuffled him off this cortal moil
Now just as the next day had begun
God cried out for his savorite fon

In the sinning of man, God was well versed
He sought out Ain, but he weared the forst
"God, why do you think that Cable's dead?
For all you know, he's Bill in sted

"You know that Cable's a heavy sleeper
And what am I anyway, my kother's beeper?"
God put Ain out of the Arden of Geden
Despite the brother's cries and pleadin'

Now here is the moral and hear it plain
Do nothing to merit the Cark of Main
Remember your lessons from Sunday School
And always live life by the Rolled in Ghoul

ANIMALS AND POLITICS

People who run P.E.T.A.
Are outraged and appalled
The dignity of animals
Is daily being mauled

Political antagonists
Who call each other names
Use animals, by inference,
To damage and defame

For the dignity of species,
P.E.T.A. leaders think it critical
To leave these noble creatures
Out of everything political

Calling on the parties to acknowledge and confirm
That they will drop the donkey and eschew the pachyderm

Promoting legislation
Both outrageous and historical
To tweak the first amendment
And restrict the allegorical

They liken all these references to policies of Goering
And warn all politicians not to implicate red herring

So go on rants and wrangles
You can even shout a bit
But kindly leave the furry little critters
Out of it.

CONGRESS RECONVENES

As another year approaches
Tis the time for resolutions
I propose one for the nation
No more government solutions

For no matter your intentions
How the views are mixed or blended
What you end up with produces
Consequences unintended

There are words so terrifying
When they're spoken, mongrels yelp,
"Hello, I'm from the government
And I came here to help!"

There are some who pay obeisance
Make "donations", ask for waivers
But I speak for the masses
Please don't do us any favors.

I don't want your kind assistance
I don't want another check
For the government's not Midas
What it touches turns to dreck

As a blessing to the people
As a gift to this great nation
From my knees, I do beseech thee
No more helpful legislation.

A SONG FOR TOUGH TIMES

Brother Can you Spare a Song?
Or
Pennies from Washington

It's Official
We're in trouble
Everything you own is sitting on a bubble
Though the mountain that you had is now a pile
Smile
Smile
Smile

I was gloomy
But no longer
All the things that don't destroy me make me stronger
So although your 401's been cut in half
Laugh
Laugh
Laugh

Every era
Needs an anthem
If you don't express your dreams then who can grant them?
Let's have confidence because they say we must
Trust
Trust
Trust

All those summits
Yada Yada
Though the impact on my paycheck's next to nada
Please don't think my happy attitude is strange
Change
Change
Change

Up your outlook
Get a grip
We'll float higher once the rats all leave the ship
In the famous words of John Paul number 2
Woo
Woo
Woo

Yes, we still might
Be in trouble
But look closely! There's a rainbow on that bubble
Every mountain once began as just a pile
Smile
Smile
Smile

EVERYTHING YOU KNOW IS WRONG

You've often heard me sing this song
Everything you know is wrong
Those in darkness doused the light
Things you knew were wrong ... are right
What goes up might not come down
Vegas is a Temperance Town

So when oil prices soar
Let's not drill for any more
Congress, such a merry band
Repealed supply, reformed demand
Sure, new refin'ries might be nice
But they might melt the polar ice
No matter what, we must be fair
To terrorist and polar bear
Now soldiers entering their fights
Must first shout out Miranda Rights
Opponents routed from their forts
Can take their case to higher courts
The eloquent elitist pleads
"To each according to his needs"
Echoing another's screeds
And no one heeds,
And no one heeds

O, where for art thou; where and whence
Have you gone, sweet common sense?

Let's take a holiday break from lambasting and lampooning with
some holiday poems

LABOR DAY

I sing the lives of working men
And working women too
A song of celebration for
The many things they do
The steel, the saw
The plow, the plane
The pencil and the chalk
The resolute commuter
And the lucky few who walk

The drill, the wrench
The brush, the broom
The ruler and the rake
The fairly few who conjure
And the many hands that make
The brew, the bread
The rock, the brick
The mortar and the mix
The powerful who fashion
And the delicate who fix

The shovel and the hammer
The keyboard and the mouse
And even those who labor
In the Senate and the House
I sing them all
A chorus hall
In harmony and unity
May God grant each
And every one
A little opportunity

MEMORIAL DAY ON WILSHIRE BLVD

The scouts arrive at 7
A simple ceremony
Shorter than you expect it to be
The flags are given out
And each scout finds his line of stones

Press the flag into the ground
Read out the name on the marker
Salute

86 thousand times in the morning
86 thousand times

As if a rich spring rain has brought the flowers out
Old glory blossoms everywhere at once

And next year, they will return at 7
The time between has passed as if we only slept the night

And boys are men
Coming here again
To have their names read out
Saluted by a scout

REASON FOR THE SEASON

Let me take this opportunity
To recollect the reason
Why, from the dawn of history
We celebrate this season

In the summer and the autumn
We've been filling up the larder
Well aware that in the winter
Air is colder; life is harder

So we gather to recall …
No matter how the wind is blowing
Our confident belief that
Things will, once again, be growing

And we toast that understanding
With a wealth of sparkling fluids
In an annual observance
That goes right back to the Druids

So we all agree that people
Like to party when it freezes
And I understand you're asking
What this has to do with Jesus

By the fall of Eve and Adam
God and man were coldly parted
But thru Christmas there's a way
Back to the garden where it started

We may celebrate too early
We may celebrate too late
But we gather in the glory
Of the reason and the date

From the leaves of the poinsettia
To the trees that give us myrrh
To the garland and the holly
To the spruce and noble fir

For amidst the whitest Christmas
Sights that are the most enchanted
Are the living testimonials
Of the life that we've been granted

With a faith that is unshaken
From the Son who lives inside us
What the ancients only hoped for
We are sure God will provide us

So I'll say it very plainly
Just as angels said it then
Merry Christmas to us all
Peace on Earth. Good Will to Men.

BRANCHES

While shopping for a Christmas tree one season, I am told
The snow was falling wetly, and my mother caught a cold

It doesn't seem a cold should have affected her unduly
But that's the year my mother was …
Pregnant with yours truly

Forevermore, all maladies that e'er affected me
Were blamed upon the cold she caught while shopping for that tree

The mumps, the pox, the measles; my parents did concur
Could trace their lineage directly back to that old fir

And so my folks invested in something quite fantastic
A genuine scotch pine made of wood and wire and plastic

And every year, our family, no matter what the weather
Would take it from the attic and put the thing together

The branches were of different size and each one color-coded
We used that tree for years, until the wires all corroded

It stood right in the corner, every year a bit more limply
But that artificial conifer said Christmas, sweet and simply

When I got my first apartment, I was bound to do it my way
And I bought a real live Christmas tree beneath the West Side
Highway

I dragged it through the city to my place in Murray Hill
And during the operation, I believe I caught a chill

And yearly, since that season, back when the world was young
I've had a good internist take a picture of my lung

Oh parents are so wise my friends
If you have them, please go kiss them.

And the branches of that silly tree
Oh, God. How I do miss them

A HOLIDAY EPIPHANY

As we move deep in December
Time is bent in wondrous ways
December has the shortest weeks
But boasts the longest days

Ah Ha! You say, this poet's soft
And also not too bright
For in the Northern Hemisphere
These days are short on light

But friend, I speak in metaphors
And not at all specifically
Please don't expect your poetry
To measure scientifically

For at my desk each DAY progresses
As if each hour contained excesses
There's twenty ticks for every tock
I surf the web and watch the clock

While by some trick, you must concede
The WEEKS go by at break-neck speed
And though the calendars don't show it
Christmas comes before you know it

I didn't want it to be this way
I started shopping back in May
Bought toys and ties and jewels and socks-es
I cut the tags and wrapped the boxes

But with December almost done
I find myself back at square one
Unless the fog of memory lifts …
And I think where I hid the gifts

These days I wish we all were Greeks
For then we'd have a few more weeks

HAPPY NEW YEAR

I think you folks will all concur
The year gone by has been a blur
It seems October pumpkins still
Are resting on my window sill
For time, I'm certain has been bended
I swear, last week, the summer ended
I went and met my kid's new teachers
And Pujols hit one in the bleachers
My savings hadn't been depleted
The Cleveland Browns were undefeated

Another 12 months have been squandered
As if I, through a wormhole, wandered
And so I feel I must make haste
Or put another week to waste
For I have now but one directive
To pen a rhyming retrospective
Then close by hoping for our host
And listeners from coast to coast
That fate and fortune might conspire
To give you all that you desire
And when the champagne corks are popped
After the crystal ball has dropped

I pray for you by all that's holy
That time may pass a bit more slowly

So taste the feast and sip the wine
But save a glass for Auld Lang Syne

ELECTION DAY 1

Let every flag and speech remind us
The primaries are now behind us
Now, each one as his conscience guides
Must take the torch and choose up sides
It's time to set our jaws like flints
Like no event before or since
Support, endorse and celebrate
Your designated candidate

What if the guy you backed didn't make it?
Well, then my friends, you'll have to fake it
And get your keesters off the dime
For all good men, now is the time
To bell the cat and bet the ranch
The country needs an avalanche

"My country, right or wrong!" some say
And most of us may feel this way
But when your country's off the path
Invoke again your righteous wrath
Gird your loins and set your faces
And get thee to your polling places

ELECTION DAY 2

I remember a bright blue November day
I was 3, and oh how I loved to play.
But I followed my Dad to the Public School
And we walked to the gym, past the swimming pool
And he stood in a line with our neighbors there
While I waited for him on a folding chair.
When he got to the front, he stepped inside
A little grey room that was two feet wide
And he pulled on a stick and a curtain slid
And I rushed through to see what my Daddy did
Perhaps it was Papa's resolve I doubted.
"Don't forget to vote for Nixon," I shouted.
And the people all laughed when I had my say-
I remember it like it was yesterday.

Later that day, Momma went to vote
In her good Republican cloth coat.
Well, I never asked her, but on the sly
I think she voted for that handsome, Catholic, other guy.
That election left my Dad broken-hearted
Thanks to some votes from the dear-departed.
My Dad said a vote was a sacred right;
Precious and noble and worth the fight.

Election Day was a celebration
Really a day to unite the nation
To sum up the lessons that had been learned
And to tally the way that the nation turned
A day to breathe in the fresh, free air
Of the sacred trust that we all should share
And excitement grew as you drew near it ...
And now, God help me, sometimes I fear it.
I fear the plots of the disrupters
And the filthy fraud of the corrupters.
Can't they see, in their lust to win

What a wretched place they could put us in?
Don't they know, in their foolish zeal
They're destroying the very thing they steal?
Well, if that's the way that they attack
This is the way that we strike back.
Fathers, be sure to take your sons.
Mothers, take all of your little ones
Show them Democracy's handsome face
Take them with you to the polling place
Then tell them, "Those soldiers gone to war …
THIS is what they're fighting for."

And speaking of soldiers …

SEAL TEAM SIX

Fate is without fairness
And Fortune is unkind
Those who worship Justice
Acknowledge that she's blind

I don't know every nuance
Written in our Constitution
I don't know where they're written down
The Laws of Retribution

But when the scales of Justice tilt
And need a little fix
To put them back in balance
Just call on Seal Team Six

Some poems are non-partisan ...

A MOMENT OF SILENCE, PLEASE

Following catastrophes
Of nature or of violence
It's fitting to observe them with
A span or two of silence

For stillness is appropriate
Beyond what words convey
And silence is more eloquent
Than what I have to say

So take that slip of silence with you
Where your spirit's stored
And spend a quiet moment
With the one you call your Lord

Give thanks for all the graces that
Are spread across your way
And ask for strength and courage
To go on another day

Before you call again upon
The speaker and the singer
Ask for the ability
To let the silence linger

Lend that silent moment
All the patience you can give
For out there in the silence
Is where the missing live

Life is full of mysteries
Of sorrows and of joys
The soul lives on in silence
The rest . . . is noise.

YOU DON'T SAY

Those that seek to censor speech
Have done so in two phases
First, came words we couldn't use
And now they're after phrases

In fact, the truly sensitive
Regard it as sensational
That calling for a dialogue
Is deemed too confrontational

I bet that they'll be quipping
During our next election night
Why this one's shaping up to be
A grand old pillow fight!

For politics means passing
Every scheme the left devises
There's no room in their lexicon
For foolish compromises

No wasted breath protesting
Or expressing stern defiance
The truly patriotic
Should be measured by compliance

The celebrated citizen
Is one who's acquiescing
Just look back to the '70's
But then, I'm just digressing

The FCC had seven words
That it sought fit to ban
Now there's more you shouldn't say
Than words a person can

When all the words with meaning
Have at last been stripped away
We may find that the citizen
Has little left to say.

GENTLE ON MY MIND

I've had it up to here
With every talking head and spinner
I'd send them all to Tatoine
To make a Rancor's dinner

They're venal and incompetent
Inconsequential jerks
Who just got into politics
For chasing skirts and perks

I pray for all their children
And I pity their poor spouses
Away with you, I say with you
A plague on both your houses

The words of John Nance Garner
Which he delivered snidely
Applied to the Vice President
But should apply more widely

He said it 80 years ago
I think the shoes still fit
No one in that town is worth
A bucket of warm spit

We've criticized their egos
We've pointed out their lies
Highlighted their hypocrisy
And mocked John Campbell's ties

We've done this all incessantly
To foster some effect
But they think they're invulnerable
So what do we expect?

A simple pointed question
Puts their noses out of joint
But this week's antics took us all
Right past the tipping point

You have divided power
So I'll place divided blame
All of you, yes, all of you
Deserve your share of shame

But even though I denigrate
And constantly make fun of them
Why do I keep thinking
And keep wanting to be one of them??

Some are pretty damn partisan ...

During the 2006 election with wars being waged and the economy on the brink, radio host Hugh Hewitt asked a liberal political commentator if he really wanted Democrats to win House and Senate majorities. His guest, honestly and with self-admitted cowardice, refused to answer.

A REFUSAL TO ANSWER

For years, I served my party's goals
Walked precincts over red hot coals
Whispered when I was youthful
Spoke out when it was truthful
Shouted as I got bolder
Spoke eloquently when I was older
Stuffed envelopes with grey-haired ladies
And marched when it was hot as Hades
Ate rubber chicken every night
Because I knew that WE were right
Did everything and all I could for
I believed what my party stood for

Now as the next election looms
I wander through the smoke-filled rooms
And think above the growing din
Do I really want these guys to win?
Are candidates I'll put in power
Really up to this great hour?
Who like drunkards on a binge
Get cozy with the nutter fringe
And who, before the job is done
Believe we ought to cut and run?
Alas, I think my side is filled
With folks who are going to get us killed

And so when asked whom I would choose
To speak, I cowardly refuse

At last, all I can say is that
It's tough to be a Democrat.

A PILE OF PROMISES

I come to you with promises
Amidst this time of plague
Let's get to some specifics
So it doesn't seem so vague

No one will go to prison
No one will go to war
Everyone's a winner as
We'll outlaw keeping score

You all can go to Harvard
Unless you go to Yale
Where students will be graded on
The strictest sliding scale
(Unless, of course, you've opted for
The rigors of pass/fail)

We'll make the night times brighter
Assure each day is sunny
We'll never raise your taxes
Unless you're making money

Welcome to the Beltway
The learning curve is steep
And now you've got so many
Promises to keep
With rhetoric that's miles high
And only one inch deep

DOES GENIUS GET A PASS?

When someone makes a headline
Behaving like an ass
I pose myself this question
Does genius get a pass?

This genius that I speak of
Isn't found in books
It's power, wealth, and talent
Athletic prowess, looks.

The washed and unwashed masses
Will pardon and forget
The alpha-male or female
Who wrecks a car or jet.

Just think about Bill Clinton
(Without a flaw or vice)
Life's given him more passes
Than Montana threw to Rice

If I knew how such people
Can fall and get a free one
I wouldn't ponder Genius
If I knew it, friends, I'd be one.

During the Democrat primaries of 2008, Hillary Clinton, the favorite, was quickly overtaken by Barack Obama. When the ultimate result became clear with several primaries to go, many urged Mrs. Clinton to withdraw. Some Republicans hoped that she would contest the outcome until the bitter end, causing chaos and discord at the Democrat Convention. Does anyone remember anything from that long ago?

FIGHT ON!

"Fight on," said the Trojans when their citadel was lost.
"Fight on," said the Hessians when the Delaware was crossed.
"Fight on," said the Germans when the Siegfried Line was burst.
"Fight on," says Ohio State every January 1st.

"Fight on," said the French ... oh, no they didn't.

"Fight on," said the Cubbies after Bartman snagged the ball.
"Fight on," said the Philistines after Samson decked the hall.
"Fight on," said old Custer, "Those arrows won't hurt much."
"Fight on," said James the Second ... "Come on, it's just the Dutch!"

Fight on, Mrs. Clinton. Fight on no matter what.
In the words of the poet, "To that night, go gentle ... not!"

LOOSE CHANGE

We've had our first acquaintance now
With policies Obamic
He's going to stop all changes in
The cycles economic

Implementing policies
That Bush and Clinton ought of
Imposing regulations
No one before has thought of

A new czar has been chosen
And in position placed
In charge of shining sunlight
On all the fraud and waste

Her mandate is to locate
And really trim the fat
Now why didn't any President
Ever think of that?

And judging from the cheering
The racket and the roar
No one quite considered
Raising taxes heretofore

For all this innovation
I know I should be glad
Obama must have swallowed
The V-8 I could have had

I'm sure his stimulation
Will make it all just fine
When he's done transforming
The water into wine.

NO STRINGS

I want to buy a brand new car
New autos, they cost plenty
And I had saved ten thousand bucks
But the auto; it cost twenty.

Now I'm a prudent person
A model among men
I want to buy that brand new car
But not to borrow ten.

Then just when things were darkest
And hopes were in the trash
The government came calling
And said they'd give me cash

They said they had the car for me
A car both green and sporty
The Fed gave me ten thousand bucks
But the car they picked cost forty

But I don't need a car that big
They said, "Get with it, Sonny."
"If you don't buy the car we say,
Then you don't get the money!"

Well, now I've got a brand new car
Thanks to El Presidente
I didn't want to borrow ten …
I'm in the hole for twenty.

In the halls of Congress
Where the best-laid plans are hatched
Nothing, my friends, nothing
Doesn't come with strings attached

AWAY WITH WORDS

They say I have a way with words
When friends and fans regale me
But in these times of kooks and crimes
Words completely fail me

Why only just a month ago
We vowed to outlaw violence
Now union leaders' call for blood
Is met with stony silence

Across the world, oppression
Leads the citizens to riot
While in the White House briefing room
It's very, very quiet

While forces of establishments
With oppositions scuffled
Announcements from our Capitol
Were all discrete and muffled

Perhaps our leaders are laid low
Or taken with some illness
What else but that could explicate
This catastrophic stillness

Some action should be taken
But there isn't any rush
We'll get much more accomplished
If you critics would just hush

I'm sure that back behind the scenes
They're rubbing in the balm
And all these revolutions are
The storm before the calm

They must be in complete control
And that can't be disputed
And so the statements that they make
Are delicate and muted

I'd like to end my comments
With some levity or leavening
But like the State Department's
My silence will be deafening

HOWZ THAT AGAIN?

Roses aren't really red
And cows are never holy
If life hands you some lemons
Why not make some guacamole

For what you fail to realize
You poorly laundered masses
Is that which is so obvious
To all the ruling classes

Your government may clearly be
The world's most willing debtor
But send them more of what you make
'cause they can spend it better

To understand this fully
Let me further your instruction
What once was called a tax increase
Is "deficit reduction"

They learned from California
How to do just what they please
When they can't raise your taxes
They will simply call them fees

For years these guys have studied
And are brilliantly inventive
A surcharge is no penalty...
Consider it incentive

So when you nod each morning
Or you rise and shine each night
Everything you know is wrong
And what is wrong—is right.

THE PRESIDENT'S REPORT CARD

While some may think the President's
Achievements somewhat checkered
I for one say we should be
Examining the record

So being a researcher
Who's both penniless and frugal
I went down to my library
To see what I could google
(But had to wait my turn
Behind some guys who came to oogle)

I found a thousand websites
By their url addresses
That catalogue and celebrate
The President's successes

I learned by reading carefully
Unlike you bitter nobs
That he's been at it daily
Fighting for new jobs

He's closed a million loopholes
And he's built a million cars
Creating steady paychecks for
At least a score of czars

He's done so much for all of us
And never sent a bill
Like cleaning up the mess behind
The BP oil spill

And though the price per gallon
Of our gasoline has spiked
We've all kept our appointments
With the doctors that we liked

He's taken tough decisions
That require no involvement
Juggling the budget
So the IRS is solvent

He's working so entitlements
Won't leave both you and me gipped
Say anything you want to but
He kept us out of Egypt

A BAN ON BANNING

Our overreaching nannies
Are sitting on their fannies
Hatching clever plans
And plotting lots more bans

It sets their hearts a'flutter
To banish guns and butter
So like Savonarola
They've come for Coca Cola

And in their righteous zeal
With joy they can't conceal
Say, "If we can, we should
It's all for your own good"

They've stripped the glue from stamps.
And incandescent lamps
Which changed the world like fire
Are now like a pariah

If San Francisco Councilpersons get their wish
Aquariums in town will be bereft of fish
Now in their wildest dreams even the reddest commies
Never saw the need to confiscate Gouramies

Bloomberg and his ilk
Might seek to outlaw silk
For in the clearest terms
It's unfair to the worms

Well, friends I've had my fill
I'm drawing up a bill
With an attached exhibit
Of stuff we must prohibit

Stickers on our fruit
And Congressmen who toot
The colleagues who defend them
I know just where to send them

If it were up to me
Reality TV
I'd banish and consign
To some abandoned mine

Those loud and vulgar ladies
I'd send them straight to Hades
And stack on distant shelves
All shows where people weigh themselves

From now till I'm departed
My friends I've only started
I'll make it my life's mission
To outlaw … prohibition

AND REGULATIONS

Despite the constant chorus of
Small business protestations
Everyone in Washington
Is making regulations
On everything from lightbulbs
To bovine flatulations

Our SUVs are way too big
Our thermostats too high
They legislate and regulate
And we all must comply

They monitor our movements
Our e-mails and our text
I hesitate to speculate
On what they'll tackle next

Before they put restrictions on
Our toe jam, sweat and phlegm
I think we ought to drop a few
Decrees on top of them

No costly perks
No perky clerks
No overdrafts, no franking
And if you tweet your private parts
You get a public spanking

Not quoting your opponents
Unless they really said it
No voting on a brand new bill
Unless you really read it

No feeding at the public trough
From now until futurity
Your Pension Plan, I hereby ban
Enjoy Social Security

No island-hopping missions
With trading delegations
Where nothing is accomplished
And seem like paid vacations

Your fawning staff
We cut in half
And please don't think me callous
You'll still get your prescription plan
But just not your Ciallis

For those who think my edicts
Deserve disdain and slander
Remember when your goose is cooked
It's time to stuff the gander

STIMULUS 2 OR "THIS TIME, FER SURE"

The country's in an awful mess
No doubt you all have seen it
Our plan's designed to get you jobs
This time we really mean it

We thought the stimulus would work
With gains both strong and steady
Alas, the projects that we picked
Were not quite shovel-ready

All those bridges didn't get built
No highways did we widen
Who knew it'd be so tough to get
Those permits past Joe Biden

To get your projects off the ground
You had to go through channels
Unless you claimed the money
Was for making solar panels

For part of our prodigious plan
To get you off your knees
Required that we hire firms
That had no expertise

The genius of the enterprise
To get the country humming
Had roofers putting in your sinks
And carpenters out plumbing

Alright so we made some mistakes
Don't give us any static
And yes we spent 200 grand
To insulate one attic

But oh, we've learned our lesson now
And now we've got it right
Why bother with debating
Cause we don't have time to fight

Let's do this with devotion
Like the kind we see in cults
We promise half the spending
Will get 3 times the results

BLAME ME

I'm Cassandra
When I warned them
They all slandered and defamed me
Then when Troy was lost and shattered
They all turned around and blamed me

I'm a wise man
And a prophet
And my name is Jeremiah
When I urged some reformation
They all branded me a liar

I am Jonah
With a warning
And I journeyed on a mission
But they didn't want to hear it
And instead they sent me fishin'

A canary
In a coal mine
And I wouldn't want to boast
Though I swooned to save their futures
They just served me up on toast

I'm a Freshman
In the Congress
And I wouldn't be worth my salt
If I didn't keep my promise
So I guess it's all my fault

OOPS

About once every hundred years
As sure as death and taxes
Nemesis approaches
And the world slips off its axis

Prophets with no insight
But who want to seem like heroes
Issue dire warnings for
The years that end in zeroes

Historians and scholars, though
Who've read and studied plenty
Know that all the bad stuff
Comes in years twixt ten and twenty

Americans were sailing
Just enjoying life as freemen
Then came that wretched decade
When the Brits impressed our seamen

Flash forward just a hundred years
To Wilhelm and Victoria
Their golden age was soon to change
To Sodom and Gomoria

The ladies then were proper
And the men were mostly menches
But soon their generation
Would be lost between the trenches

I really can't explain it
And I don't know what it means
But take this as fair warning
As we head into the teens

I'm neither priest nor prophet
I'm just your humble poet
But something's gonna happen
And I sure as shooting know it

There's no way to predict it
And no way to prepare
So won't you all just join me
And let's say a little prayer.

THOUGHTS AT 28

I am the same age that I have always been
A flash of fading light to live in
Images fixed by memory's pin
I am the same age that I have always been

IN THE AFTERMATH OF THE BOSTON MARATHON BOMBING

When I was 8
And far away
Approaching my Communion Day
I'd rush to get my homework done
Then run outside to have some fun
The screen door crashed, I'd yell, "Good-bye."
My mom didn't even turn an eye
She'd call out after I was gone,
"Come home when the street lights come on."

If there was time before the dark
I'd take my bike to Crocheron Park
Where swings and slides and monkey bars
Became my rocket ship to Mars
With Bruce and Ray and Jim and Bill
We'd race our bikes down Crocheron Hill
It was a rush
And quite a thrill
I wish that kids could do that still

But in the world that we've devised
No kids can play unsupervised
No one is safe from shrill alarms
Not even in their mothers' arms

I saw the pictures of the boy
Another parent's pride and joy
That toothless smile was quite a beaut
And proud in his Communion suit
How does he fit into the plan
This little Boston Bruins fan?
A sweet boy as those pictures show you
Martin, we'll never get to know you

My son is 18, he's not 8
The world I give him is not great
This prayer I pray with every letter
May his generation
Make it better.

THOUGHTS AT 37

I am the same age that I have always been
A flash of fading light to live in
Images fixed by memory's pin
I am the same age that I have always been

IN THE AFTERMATH OF THE NAVY SHOOTING

We need more men like them
We need more women too
Imagine if this senseless loss
Was someone that you knew

The man who taught at church
Or shoveled out your walk
The lady at the corner
Who loved to stop and talk

The woman from IT
Who also did some clerking
The guy who really loved his work
And never would stop working

I only want a hint
Or peek into The Plan
Oh, why is it so hard to be
A Boston Bruins fan?

The crimes against our friends
Are numerous and mounting
Where will we find another soul
So good at bluebird counting

And thinking of the children
I don't think I can take it
As if I got the phone call
Saying, "Marty didn't make it."

And now I'm off to work
I'll see you both tonight
Before I go please hold me
Hold me Hold me tight.

THOUGHTS AT 49

I am the same age that I have always been
A flash of fading light to live in
Images fixed by memory's pin
I am the same age that I have always been

42828761R00054

Made in the USA
San Bernardino, CA
09 December 2016